Peanuts
Lentils
Peas
Beans
Peanuts
Lentils

PLANTS
WE EAT

Peas
Beans
Peanuts
Lentils
Peas
Beans
Peanuts
Lentils
Peas
Beans
Peanuts
Lentils
Peas

Spill the Beans and Pass the Peanuts

Legumes

Meredith Sayles Hughes

Lerner Publications Company/Minneapolis

Check out the author's website at www.foodmuseum.com/hughes

Website address: www.lernerbooks.com

Designers: Steven P. Foley, Réna Dehler
Editor: Amy M. Boland
Photo Researcher: Kirsten Frickle

LIBRARY OF CONGRESS CATALOGING-IN-
PUBLICATION DATA

Hughes, Meredith Sayles.
    Spill the beans and pass the peanuts : legumes / by
Meredith Sayles Hughes.
        p. cm. — (Plants we eat)
    Includes index.
    Summary: Presents information on the history,
production, and uses of several popular members of the
legume family: peanuts, lentils, peas, and beans,
particularly soybeans. Includes recipes.
    ISBN 0–8225–2834–7 (lib. bdg. : alk. paper)
    1. Legumes—Juvenile literature. 2. Cookery
(Legumes)—Juvenile literature. [1. Legumes.] I. Title.
II. Series.
SB177.L45H84 1999
583'.74—dc21   98–29663

Manufactured in the United States of America
1 2 3 4 5 6 – MP – 04 03 02 01 00 99

The glossary on page 77 gives definitions of
words shown in **bold type** in the text.

Contents

Introduction

Plants make all life on our planet possible. They provide the oxygen we breathe and the food we eat. Think about a burger and fries. The meat comes from cattle, which eat plants. The fries are potatoes cooked in oil from soybeans, corn, or sunflowers. The burger bun is a wheat product. Ketchup is a mixture of tomatoes, herbs, and corn syrup or the sugar from sugarcane. How about some onions or pickle relish with your burger?

How Plants Make Food

By snatching sunlight, water, and carbon dioxide from the atmosphere and mixing them together—a complex process called **photosynthesis**—green plants create food energy. The raw food energy is called glucose, a simple form of sugar. From this storehouse of glucose, each plant produces fats, carbohydrates, and proteins—the elements that make up the bulk of the foods humans and animals eat.

Sunlight peeks through the branches of a plant-covered tree in a tropical rain forest, where all the elements exist for photosynthesis to take place.

First we eat, then we do everything else.

—M. F. K. Fisher

Plants offer more than just food. They provide the raw materials for making the clothes you're wearing and the paper in books, magazines, and newspapers. Much of what's in your home comes from plants—the furniture, the wallpaper, and even the glue that holds the paper on the wall. Eons ago plants created the gas and oil we put in our cars, buses, and airplanes. Plants even give us the gum we chew.

On the Move

Although we don't think of plants as beings on the move, they have always been pioneers. From their beginnings as algaelike creatures in the sea to their movement onto dry land about 400 million years ago, plants have colonized new territories. Alone on the barren rock of the earliest earth, plants slowly established an environment so rich with food, shelter, and oxygen that some forms of marine life took up residence on dry land. Helped along by birds who scattered seeds far and wide, plants later sped up their travels, moving to cover most of our planet.

Early in human history, when few people lived on the earth, gathering food was everyone's main activity. Small family groups were nomadic, venturing into areas that offered a source of water, shelter, and foods such as fruits, nuts, seeds, and small game animals. After they had eaten up the region's food sources, the family group moved on to another spot. Only when people noticed that food plants were renewable—that the berry bushes would bear fruit again and that grasses gave forth seeds year after year—did family groups begin to settle in any one area for more than a single season.

Organisms that behave like algae—small, rootless plants that live in water

It's a Fact!

The term *photosynthesis* comes from Greek words meaning "putting together with light." This chemical process, which takes place in a plant's leaves, is part of the natural cycle that balances the earth's store of carbon dioxide and oxygen.

Native Americans were the first peoples to plant crops in the Americas.

Domestication of plants probably began as an accident. Seeds from a wild plant eaten at dinner were tossed onto a trash pile. Later a plant grew there, was eaten, and its seeds were tossed onto the pile. The cycle continued on its own until someone noticed the pattern and repeated it deliberately. Agriculture radically changed human life. From relatively small plots of land, more people could be fed over time, and fewer people were required to hunt and gather food. Diets shifted from a broad range of wild foods to a more limited but more consistent menu built around one main crop such as wheat, corn, cassava, rice, or potatoes. With a stable food supply, the world's population increased and communities grew larger. People had more time on their hands, so they turned to refining their skills at making tools and shelter and to developing writing, pottery, and other crafts.

Plants We Eat

This series examines the wide range of plants people around the world have chosen to eat. You will discover where plants came from, how they were first grown, how they traveled from their original homes, and where they have become important and why. Along the way, each book looks at the impact of certain plants on society and discusses the ways in which these food plants are sown, harvested, processed, and sold. You will also discover that some plants are key characters in exciting high-tech stories. And there are plenty of opportunities to test recipes and to dig into other hands-on activities.

The series Plants We Eat divides food plants into a variety of informal categories. Some plants are prized for their seeds, others for their fruits, and some for their underground roots, tubers, or bulbs. Many plants offer leaves or stalks for good eating. Humans convert some plants into oils and others into beverages or flavorings. Plants that give us seeds packed into pods are called legumes or leguminous plants. The edible seeds are collectively known as **pulses.** This extensive grouping of plants, with origins both in the Eastern and Western Hemispheres, provides protein-loaded food for both people and animals. Legumes include **ornamental** vines like the wisteria and trees such as the redbud and mimosa. And several of its members are industrial stars as well.

Many of these plants grow like vines. They may wind their own stalks around other plants or poles on their climb toward the sun, or they may cling with tiny tendrils. Some, like the scarlet runner bean, burst with gloriously bright flowers that resemble the blossoms of sweet peas. All legumes depend on their flowers, whether showy or not, to produce their seeds. In *Spill the Beans and Pass the Peanuts: Legumes*, we'll take a closer look at peanuts, lentils, peas, and beans, with a special emphasis on the soybean.

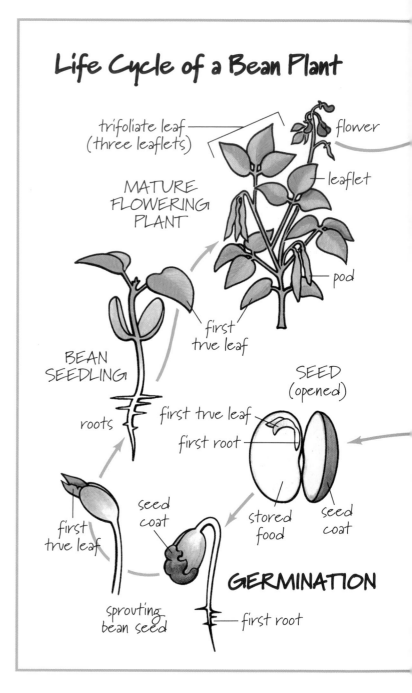

Life Cycle of a Bean Plant

trifoliate leaf (three leaflets)

flower

leaflet

MATURE FLOWERING PLANT

pod

first true leaf

BEAN SEEDLING

SEED (opened)

roots

first true leaf

first root

first true leaf

seed coat

stored food

seed coat

sprouting bean seed

GERMINATION

first root

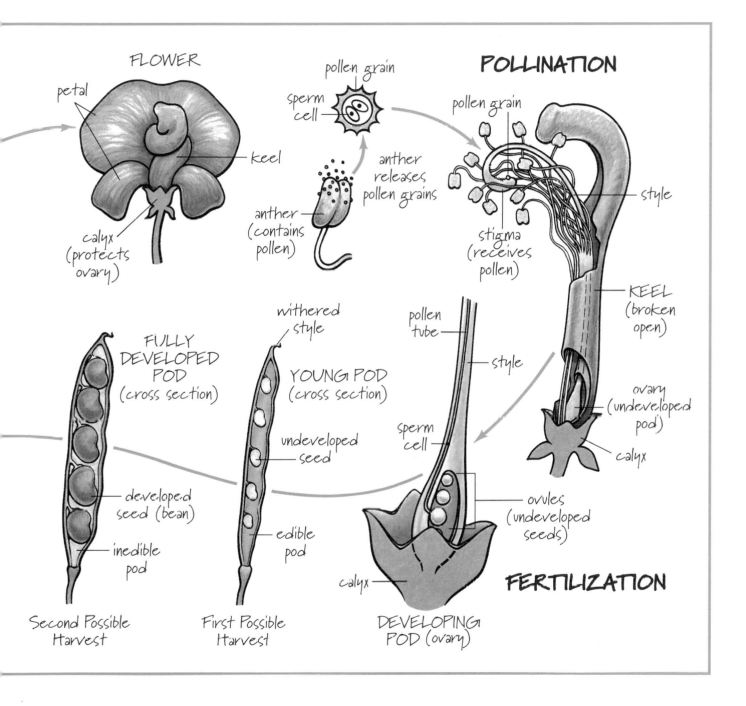

FLOWER

petal

keel

calyx
(protects
ovary)

pollen grain

sperm cell

anther
releases
pollen grains

anther
(contains
pollen)

POLLINATION

pollen grain

style

stigma
(receives
pollen)

KEEL
(broken
open)

ovary
(undeveloped
pod)

calyx

FULLY
DEVELOPED
POD
(cross section)

withered
style

YOUNG POD
(cross section)

pollen
tube

style

sperm
cell

undeveloped
seed

developed
seed (bean)

inedible
pod

edible
pod

ovules
(undeveloped
seeds)

calyx

FERTILIZATION

Second Possible
Harvest

First Possible
Harvest

DEVELOPING
POD (ovary)

Peanuts

[*Arachis hypogaea*]

Every elephant's favorite legume, the peanut is not a nut, nor is it a pea, although it is related to the pea family. The peanut somewhat resembles clover, its shorter relative, with bright green leaves, yellow flowers, and multiple stalks. Its pod, or shell, resembles that of a pea, and its seeds sit tightly together as do peas in a pod. Unlike a pea plant, however, the peanut grows in a most curious manner. The peanut puts forth flowers low on the stem. As the flowers fall, the stem on which the pod forms, known as the peg, droops down toward the soil. Then the peg pokes itself into the ground and there the pod ripens, forming peanuts within the shell.

Most varieties of peanut contain two seeds per pod.

No man in the world has more courage than the man who can stop after eating one peanut.

—Channing Pollock

Researchers think that the peanut plant growing in the wild thousands of years ago probably produced its fruit above ground in the usual way. Why did it change and make a beeline for the soil? Perhaps the earliest, ancestral peanut plant was repeatedly devastated by locusts, grasshoppers, or other insects. By burying its reproductive parts underground, safe from munching mouths, the peanut may have protected itself from destruction.

The peanut is native to South America, probably from the lowlands of present-day Bolivia. The abundance of wild peanut varieties in this region points to the plant's origins there. Domesticated peanut plants

Family Matters

To keep things straight in the huge families of plants and animals, scientists classify and name living things by grouping them according to shared features within each of seven major categories. The categories are kingdom, division or phylum, class, order, family, genus, and species. Species share the most features in common, while members of a kingdom or division share far fewer traits. This system of scientific classification and naming is called taxonomy. Scientists refer to plants and animals by a two-part Latin or Greek term made up of the genus and the species name. The genus name comes first, followed by the species name. When talking about a genus that has more than one commonly cultivated species, such as *Phaseolus* (beans), we'll use only the genus name in the chapter heading. In the discussions about specific legumes, we'll list the two-part species name. Look at the peanut's taxonomic name on page 10. Can you figure out to what genus the peanut belongs? And to what species?

A Bolivian farmer harvests his peanut crop by hand.

were growing in modern-day Brazil and on islands in the Caribbean Sea about 5,000 years ago. At that time, the plant flourished in the coastal areas of Peru, where peanuts were a popular snack food. Archaeologists (scientists who study ancient cultures) in that part of Peru have unearthed broad plazas littered with ancient peanut shells, much like a baseball stadium after a game.

The Chimu people, whose culture flourished on the northern coast of Peru starting in the A.D. 700s, made pottery depicting the peanut. Actual peanuts have been found in tombs of the period. The Nazca people, who succeeded the Chimu in northern Peru, included peanut images in their pottery, an indication that the food was of cultural, as well as agricultural, interest.

The peanut's early expedition beyond its American home was probably with the Portuguese colonists of Brazil on South America's eastern coast. In the 1500s, Portuguese ships carried peanuts, along with other New World foods, across the Atlantic Ocean to Portuguese slave-trading outposts in West Africa. The Portuguese planted these new foods in Africa to provide ample, cheap food for Africans. The Portuguese then shipped the Africans to the peanut's home turf—the Caribbean islands and Brazil—to work colonial plantations as slaves.

The Spaniards first noticed the peanut in Peru around 1530. From there they brought the plant to Spain and on to their Asian outposts, such as the Malay Peninsula and the Philippines. Established in much of Asia and Africa and in Spain by the early 1600s, the peanut arrived in North America somewhat later. Most evidence indicates that African slaves brought the peanut plant to North America sometime in the early to mid-1600s. Many of the Africans would have been familiar with peanuts, cultivated in their homeland since the mid-1500s. Whether these people somehow carried the plant themselves or whether their captors sent it to be planted in North America is not known.

Goober, a U.S. slang term for "peanut," derives from nguba. The Gedda people of West Africa use the word to indicate a type of ground nut resembling a peanut.

English immigrants to North America began settling in the colony of Virginia in 1607. They brought the first African slaves to Virginia in 1619.

The New Americans

In the late 1400s and early 1500s, Europeans set sail on voyages to find a sea route to the spices and other riches of India and Southeast Asia. In 1492, while directing a Spanish voyage, Christopher Columbus stumbled onto the Americas.

In 1500 Portuguese explorer Pedro Cabral, seeking a route around Africa to Asia, bumped into what would become Brazil, the only area on the continent settled by the Portuguese. All the rest was under Spanish rule. Other European countries, including Britain and France, eventually claimed holdings in the Americas, too.

But Europeans didn't just hold onto the land. They sent settlers, some of whom established huge plantations. Spanish and Portuguese plantation owners ran their enormous farms with free labor—at first they forced local Native Americans to work for them, and later they brought Africans to work as slaves. Eventually independent nations of free citizens arose from these colonies. Kitchen lore from all three cultures—Native American, African, and European—blended into cooking traditions that persist to this day.

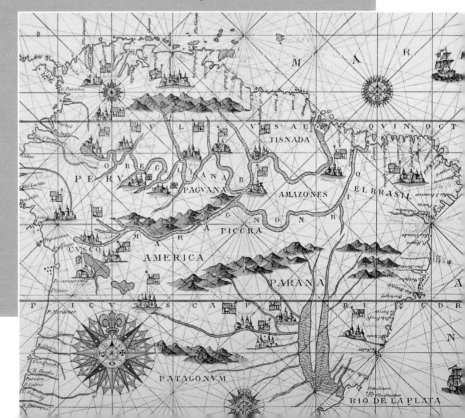

This Spanish map from 1582 shows a few European outposts in northeastern South America.

Slaves pick cotton on a North Carolina plantation just before the U.S. Civil War.

Because written evidence from the slaves themselves is limited, we don't know how widely they grew peanuts or how much of a role the legume played in their daily diet. It is quite possible that at first the peanut was planted in small gardens alongside the slave cabins. Plantation owners, perhaps observing the slaves' use of the plant, became interested in peanuts. The owners began planting peanuts primarily as food for fattening pigs.

Peanut growing was concentrated mainly in the American South (the present-day states of Alabama, Georgia, Louisiana, Mississippi, North Carolina, South Carolina, and parts of Florida, Virginia, Arkansas, Tennessee, and Texas). By 1800 South Carolina

had established some commercial peanut farms. North Carolina began growing peanuts about 1818, and Virginia followed in the 1840s. During the U.S. Civil War (1861–1865), soldiers on both sides ate rations of peanuts. Troops on the march could easily carry this nourishing and portable food in pockets or packs. After the war, soldiers from the North brought their peanut habit back home.

After the Civil War, peanuts began to replace cotton, once a major source of income for Southern farmers, as a **cash crop.** Cotton declined partly because during the war, when U.S. cotton was not available, customers had found other sources. Farmers

The Peanut Man

George Washington Carver, a plant scientist in the early part of the 1900s, saw in the peanut a potent industrial force. He turned peanuts not only into butter and oil but also into more than 300 manufactured products ranging from shoe polish to shaving cream. Carver's enthusiasm for the peanut as a culinary delight as well as an industrial star led him to invite a group of businesspeople to his home at Tuskegee Institute in Tuskegee, Alabama. There he served his guests a meal made entirely of peanuts, starting with peanut soup and moving to peanut dessert followed by peanut coffee.

also grew increasingly aware that cotton was hard on the soil. The peanut stepped in to take cotton's place.

By the 1870s, the peanut was a popular snack food, roasted by street vendors or sold at sporting events and circuses. But as demand soared, technology couldn't keep up. At this time, peanut planting and harvesting were done by hand, and many times the results were sloppy. Customers found stems and bits of shell in their peanuts. In about 1900, inventors created machines to help with planting, harvesting, shelling, and cleaning. These modernizations ultimately turned the peanut into a multimillion-dollar industry in the South.

Roasted peanuts as a treat for circus goers and elephants alike first appeared for sale at P. T. Barnum's circus, "The Greatest Show on Earth," in about 1871.

Two women sell groundnut paste—otherwise known as peanut butter—at a market in Accra, the capital of the West African country of Ghana.

The World Peanut

China and India grow most of the world's peanuts, and Asian people eat more peanuts than anyone else in the world. Asia grows about 72 percent of the world's crop of peanuts, Africa about 20 percent, and North and Central America combined produce about 7.5 percent. In all, 108 countries grow peanuts.

West Africa was a peanut power from the late 1500s, when the Portuguese introduced the crop, through the mid-1970s. In Kano, Nigeria, for example, workers in the railyards used to pile sacks of peanuts into pyramids taller than the city's buildings. From there trains took the sacks to the seaport of Lagos for transport to markets in Europe. In 1975 a disease called rosette devastated production. European buyers turned to peanut suppliers outside Africa because they could no longer count on West Africa to grow enough. The economic hardship on many African countries has been profound.

Rosette, a plant disease carried by tiny insects called aphids, remains a threat in Africa.

In the East African nation of Malawi, peanut growers are traditionally **subsistence farmers** who raise peanuts for their own use on tiny plots. Shortage of seed is always a problem for these small farmers. One reason is because people living at a subsistence level sometimes find it hard to set peanuts aside. They might run out of food and then nibble away at the seed stock they will need for planting. Another reason is tied to the overall drop in Africa's peanut production. Many peanut-seed farmers switched to other crops or abandoned agriculture altogether. As a result, seed stocks are scarce and expensive.

Another effect of the downturn in peanut production has been a nutritional shortfall. For many rural Africans, peanuts are the primary source of much-needed oil. Without adequate oil in the diet, people cannot absorb and use the vitamins available in vegetables. Vitamin A deficiency, for instance, is a serious health problem for African children living at poverty level. Lack of vitamin A causes eye illnesses as well as other ailments, leaving children weak and vulnerable to deadly diseases.

The importance of the peanut in Africa for food and income has led to increased efforts by international development groups to help bring back peanut production across West Africa. Scientists have developed rosette-resistant varieties. Local farmers are testing newly created strains of peanuts that combine drought resistance with high productivity. The ultimate goal is for peanuts once again to be a cash crop for African farmers.

In the 1960s—before a disease called rosette ruined West Africa's peanut industry—many Africans, such as this Senegalese man, worked in the business.

It's a Fact!

In China, where much of the peanut cultivation is done by hand, farmers put plastic mulch on peanut fields to keep temperatures warm around each plant, to keep back weeds, and to retain moisture.

Peanut Particulars

Even though peanuts come in hundreds of varieties suited for the world's different soils and climates, there are only four basic types of peanuts. The variety called runner, a high yielder with uniform kernel size, is the peanut most frequently grown in the United States. The Virginia peanut claims the largest kernels and is usually chosen for roasting and processing in the shell. The small-kerneled Spanish, primarily planted in Oklahoma and Texas, is high in oil content. Spanish peanuts frequently go into candies, such as peanut brittle, and into peanut butter. Valencia, a sweet peanut, often produces three small seeds to the shell and is New Mexico's pride.

Growing and Selling

Commercial peanut operations plant one crop per season. In industrialized growing areas, specialized machines drop seed peanuts into sandy, warm soil about two inches deep in rows three feet apart. One peanut falls into the ground every three to four inches. After two weeks, the first leaves of the tiny peanut plants push through the soil. In another three to four weeks, the peanut plant blooms and sends its pegs back underground, where the light-brown, pod-like hulls develop with the peanut kernels inside. In two more months, the peanuts reach maturity and are ready to harvest.

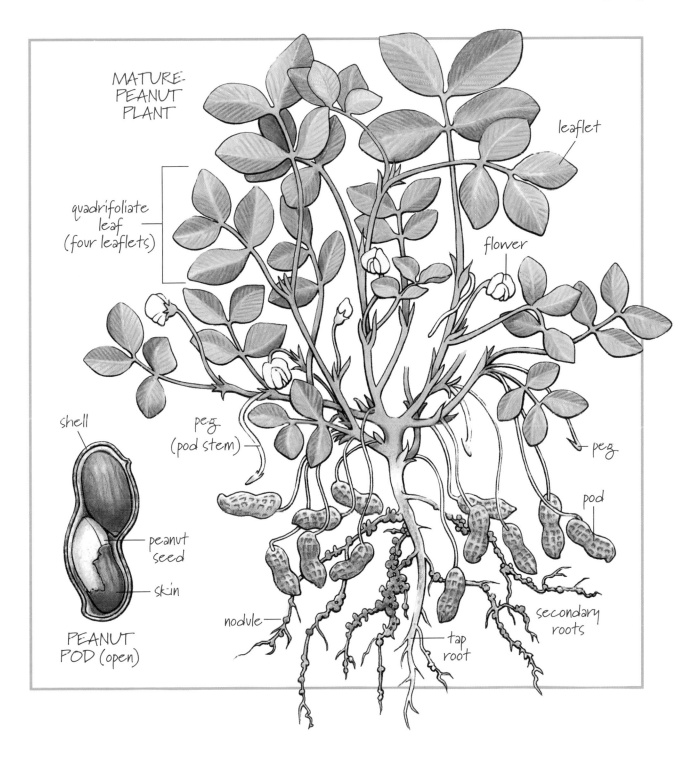

MATURE
PEANUT
PLANT

leaflet

quadrifoliate
leaf
(four leaflets)

flower

shell

peg
(pod stem)

peg

peanut
seed

pod

skin

PEANUT
POD (open)

nodule

tap
root

secondary
roots

When the plants are fully grown and the fields sufficiently dry, the farmer drives in a machine with four- to six-inch digger blades that slice deep underground, cutting major roots and lifting the plants from the soil. Directly behind the blades is a device that takes the plants from the soil, shakes the dirt loose, and then turns the plants over and places them back down on the ground—leafy side down—to dry in the sun for two days. This stage is important because peanuts full of moisture—as much as 50 percent when they are picked—will spoil quickly.

Next, combines enter the field. These machines separate the peanuts from the vine and shoot the goobers into a hopper (carrier) on top of the combine. To finish off the

A peanut farmer uses a specialized tractor to pull his plants out of the ground in the first stage of harvesting *(above)*. A combine dumps the harvested crop into a truck *(left)*.

curing (drying), workers load the peanuts into special wagons. Warm air blows through the floor of each wagon, drying the peanuts until they have a moisture content of 10 percent.

At this point, trucks haul the peanuts to huge, dry-storage warehouses, where they will await sale to **brokers** or growers' associations. It's the buyer's job to process the peanuts. First, the peanuts travel on a conveyor belt to a cleaning machine that removes dirt and leaves. The equipment may trim the stem ends if the peanuts are to be sold in the shell, the fate of about 10 percent of the U.S. crop.

Those peanuts headed for further processing go into rotating drums, where the shells rub against one another and pop open. Another machine separates the kernels from the hulls.

At this stage, most shelled peanuts are warmed and their papery skins rubbed off on large rollers. This step is called blanching, a term that means "making white." Other machines clean the kernels; sort them by color, size, and quality; and bag the peanuts. Manufacturers buy the processed bulk peanuts and turn them into the products we buy in the store.

Burlap sacks of processed North Carolina peanuts are ready to be sold to customers.

Jimmy Carter, who was president of the United States from 1977 to 1981, was raised and still lives in Plains, Georgia, the heart of peanut country.

The Peanut State

In the United States, Georgia is top peanut. Georgia produces almost half of the country's peanuts each year and boasts Jimmy Carter, the only U.S. president to grow up on a peanut farm. About three-quarters of Georgia's peanuts become peanut butter, and North Americans eat millions of pounds of the concoction. All told, peanuts generate about $500 million for Georgia farmers each year.

Eating Global Goober Peas

The rich flavor of the peanut is so distinctive that dishes prepared worldwide all share a common character. Even North American peanut-butter sandwiches belong to this large group.

In Peru, Bolivia, Ecuador, and other parts of South America, peanut sauces are common. A typical sauce combines chopped hard-boiled egg, cheese, olives, chilies, and spices into a rich, thick sauce often served on freshly boiled potatoes. One such Peruvian dish, a meal in itself, is called *papas arequipeñas. Vatapa de galinha,* a Brazilian chicken stew with a sauce made of coconut milk and peanuts, is a favorite food in the state of Bahia on Brazil's eastern coast.

People enjoy the peanut in much of Africa, too. In the southern African nation of Zimbabwe, people roast the legumes without oil and add salt for a high-protein snack. *Shiro wat,* a chili-laced peanut stew from Ethiopia, is hot and spicy. People traditionally serve it on rice or with millet cakes. Kenyans make *kunde,* a stew with beans and ground peanuts that's often served with a corn pudding. In Malawi and Zambia, as well as in other parts of Africa, peanuts are the prime ingredient in a tomato-rich relish that can be served hot or cold. Cooks from Mali in West Africa make *kuli-kuli,* fried peanut cakes, from freshly ground peanut paste. Peanuts even turn up in a dessert—egg yolks, sugar,

It's a Fact!

Diners can order peanut soup, an African dish, in the restaurant adjoining Mount Vernon, George Washington's home in northern Virginia. Slave cooks in American colonial kitchens probably introduced the soup, a food they had made for their families back home in Africa.

A peanut-butter-and-jelly sandwich makes a nutritious meal. Peanuts contain 26 percent protein, the body's basic building material.

A group of diners in the Chinese city of Hong Kong enjoys dishes stir-fried in peanut oil.

and ground peanuts cooked up into a thick pudding—in the East African country of Mozambique.

Asian cooks love their peanuts, too. *Katjang saus*, a spicy peanut sauce served with grilled meats and rice, is an Indonesian specialty. Made from ginger, chilies, garlic, ground peanuts, limes, shrimp paste, and shallots, this Southeast Asian sauce would taste somewhat familiar to diners in South America and Africa as well. A similar Malay sauce adds coconut milk as a key ingredient and, poured over a plate of lightly cooked vegetables, creates a dish called *gado-gado*. Indonesians make thin wafers of chopped peanuts, enjoy boiled peanuts topped with a chili sauce, and strew chopped, roasted peanuts on a variety of salads. People in Thailand make a salad of green papayas and roasted peanuts. Many Thai dishes are garnished with a sprinkling of chopped, roasted peanuts. The Vietnamese

Counterfeit Coffee

Peanuts, as well as soybeans and certain grains, have long been used as substitutes for coffee. In times of coffee shortages, or for people who want "coffee" without the caffeine, legumes do the trick. To make fake coffee, people dry, roast, grind, and brew the peanuts, much as is done with true coffee beans. Sometimes flavored with ground chicory (the root of a member of the daisy family), peanut coffee tastes just like, uh . . . poffee?

mix grated root vegetables with peanuts in yet another salad combination. Vietnamese children sometimes eat boiled peanuts as a breakfast food.

China could well be called "the Big Peanut," so important is the legume to this country. People use peanut oil for frying—the oil is mild, colorless, and, best of all, does not smoke at high temperatures. Chinese cooks deep-fry peanuts in their own oil, mix them into stir-fries, and boil them like beans. Ground finely and mixed with sugar, peanuts also make a filling for assorted sweets.

In India peanuts mixed with other dried legumes make *bhel poori*, a simple snack similar to trail mix. Peanuts thicken Indian curries, stews, and soups.

An Indian girl roasts peanuts over a simple wood-burning stove.

Workers grind goobers at a Kenyan peanut-butter factory.

In the United States, particularly in the South, peanuts are a favorite ingredient. Peanut soup—a creamy specialty from colonial times—remains a Southern standby, along with peanut brittle and peanut-crust pies. Many Southerners enjoy fresh peanuts boiled in the shell in salt water. Prepared this way, peanuts are soft, moist, and extremely salty—not at all like crisp, dry, roasted peanuts. Boiled peanuts remind us that we're eating something closer to peas, not nuts, after all.

Peanut butter, of course, sits in nearly every kitchen in the United States. But did you know that it's one of the earliest peanut products? Some 2,000 years ago, the Aztec people of central Mexico invented the spread. These days peanut-butter manufacturers grind roasted peanuts and then add vegetable oil, a sweetener such as corn syrup, and salt. Peanut-butter purists, however, often grind their own, adding nothing. The average American eats close to three pounds of peanut butter every year!

Peanut Better

Every bit of the peanut plant is useful. The roots, like those of other leguminous plants, form nodules (little bumps) that absorb nitrogen from the air and then replenish the soil with **nitrates,** chemicals that help plants grow. After the harvest is over, farmers plow the vines into the ground to act as fertilizer, too. Ground peanut shells turn up in building materials, such as wallboard, and as added roughage or fiber for cattle feed. Some brands of kitty litter contain hulls, as do fake fireplace logs. Peanut oil not suitable for cooking can go into soap, shaving cream, cosmetics, paint, and even an explosive called nitroglycerin.

And there's also "Wonder Peanut." A University of Florida plant breeder developed this peanut, which contains 80 percent oleic acid instead of the usual 50 percent. Oleic

Reese's!

Billing itself as "the world's best-selling candy bar," Reese's Peanut Butter Cup has been a success almost since its creation. The inventor, H. B. Reese, started out making various candies first in his kitchen and then in a rented basement in Hershey, Pennsylvania. Quite soon he was a modest success. But in 1928, Reese hit the jackpot when he surrounded peanut butter with milk chocolate. Selling for one cent apiece, the Reese's Cup was so successful that by 1941 Reese had eliminated all his other candies in order to concentrate on the cup. From the beginning, he bought the chocolate from the Hershey Company, which owns Reese's Peanut Butter Cup.

acid seems to reduce cholesterol, which can form a dangerous buildup on the insides of people's blood vessels. Oil made from this special peanut would be a healthier choice for cooking.

Finally, consider *Arachis glabrata* Benth. Originating in Brazil and known as the perennial peanut, this plant may be an environmental hero. People in warmer areas of the United States use the perennial peanut as ground cover or mix it with other forage for grazing animals. But the plant's newest application may be with the citrus crop of southwestern Florida. University of Florida horticulturists (crop scientists) have planted perennial peanuts between citrus trees for several reasons. The peanuts absorb runoff water from the trees, thereby preventing soil erosion. The peanuts also replenish the soil with nitrates for the trees and require no additional fertilization for themselves, thus protecting underground water from fertilizer contamination.

A thick turf of perennial peanuts grows between rows of citrus trees in southwestern Florida. The small, yellow flowers spring up as weeds on lawns throughout the state *(inset)*.

Dig In!

SALSA DE MANÍ (PEANUT SAUCE)
(¾ CUP)

3 tablespoons minced onion

3 tablespoons butter

1 tablespoon minced jalapeño pepper (fresh or canned)

1 tomato, peeled and coarsely chopped

½ cup ground or finely chopped roasted peanuts

3 to 4 tablespoons water

salt and pepper, to taste

To peel the tomato, use a sharp paring knife to cut a small X on the bottom. Put the tomato in boiling water for about 30 seconds. Remove the tomato with tongs and place it in a bowl of cold water. The skin will slip off easily.

At medium heat, sauté the onion in butter for 2 minutes. Add the jalapeño pepper and the tomato. Continue cooking about 5 minutes until the sauce becomes mushy. Add the peanuts and mix well. Remove from the heat and add the water a little at a time until the sauce is the desired thickness. Season with salt and pepper. Put this sauce on boiled potatoes for a treat enjoyed regularly in Ecuador.

Lentils
[*Lens culinaris*]

Among the world's oldest cultivated foods, lentils are actually some of the most digestible legumes—and the quickest to cook, too. The little lentil comes in colors ranging from orange to pink to grayish green. Lentil pods grow on a viny, green plant with long, thin leaves.

Lentils probably first appeared in present-day north-eastern Iraq. At Qalat Jarmo, Iraq, archaeologists have found lentils nearly 9,000 years old. Researchers in Turkey have found 7,000-year-old containers of lentils marked as having been grown in Sumeria (modern-day Iraq). Researchers have found lentils in Greece as well, at a site called Argissa-Magula, a dwelling place that flourished 8,500 years ago. At some early date, India aquired the plant, too.

People around the world eat lentils of various colors.

This vegetable is best eaten only by those with strong stomachs.

—from the *Diccionario de Cocina,* 1845

Ancient Egyptians, who built and decorated this tomb in the old city of Thebes (near modern-day Qena on the Nile River), grew and ate lentils.

Lentils were well known to the Egyptians, who grew them at least 5,000 years ago. Scientists found an offering of mashed lentils in one Egyptian tomb. The pulses somehow found their way across the Mediterranean Sea and into Europe. During the Bronze Age (roughly from 3000 to 1000 B.C.), people cultivated lentils along the Danube River, which stretches from the Black Forest of Germany to the shores of the Black Sea.

Nutritionally rich yet abundant and easy to grow, lentils have always been cheap—the food of the poor. Lentils were a staple food in ancient Greece and Rome for poor and rich people alike, though the wealthy were snobbishly uneasy about enjoying such an inexpensive food. The Romans ate so many lentils that they

The Stone, Bronze, and Iron Ages are very rough, overlapping segments of time in history. The names refer to the material most people used to make tools at the time.

had to import tons of them from Egypt. Ships carrying the tiny pulses regularly sailed from Alexandria in Egypt to Roman ports in Italy. At the time of the Roman emperor Caligula, at the beginning of the first century A.D., a stone obelisk carved in Egypt came to Rome on a specially built ship. More than 2.8 million pounds of Egyptian red lentils the packing material of ancient times—cushioned the huge stone. The monument still stands in front of St. Peter's Basilica in Vatican City, but the lentils that protected it have long since been eaten.

By the time the Middle Ages (roughly between A.D. 500 and 1500) rolled around, people across Europe were eating well on lentils. Alas, many still looked down on the pulses as poor people's food, and chroniclers of the time went out of their way to dump on the little lentil. In 1475 an Italian writer named Platina wrote that lentils were "the worst of all vegetables."

Despite the bad press, when lentils reached France, they were eventually accepted by influential people. A French surgeon named Ambroise Pare claimed that lentils were effective against smallpox, a disease that claimed many lives in the 1500s. Marie de Sévigné, a noblewoman close to the court of King Louis XIV (who ruled France from 1643 to 1715), loved lentil soup made from lentils grown in Nantes, a town in France's Loire River Valley. Nantes lentils

The obelisk in St. Peter's Square is a landmark in Vatican City, an independent country completely within the city limits of Rome. Vatican City is the spiritual and governmental center of the Roman Catholic Church.

must have grown in esteem. Louis XV, France's king from 1715 to 1774, named them *lentilles à la reine* (the queen's lentils) for his wife, Maria Leszczyńska—a native of Poland, where lentils were a favorite food. Lentilles à la reine are still France's most famous lentil dish.

At some point thereafter, the people of the royal court moved on to another trendy food. The wealthy ceased to admire the lentil and fed it instead to their horses. The majority of the French people were poor, however, and were happy to have lentils at any time. Beginning about 1788, bread—which constituted 75 percent of the average person's diet—became scarce and expensive. Grain harvests were poor for several years, so lentils may have kept some of the peasantry alive. After the chaos of the French Revolution (1789–1799), food supplies were in disarray, and lentils were once more welcome in all French kitchens.

Maria Leszczyńska, namesake of the French lentil dish lentilles à la reine

The Palouse region in the northwestern United States raises **98** percent of all U.S. lentils, or about **67,500** tons annually. This greenish-brown variety *(inset)* is commonly found in U.S. supermarkets.

From France to the Americas

In the meantime, French trappers and explorers in present-day eastern Canada were quickly followed by missionaries intent on converting the native people to Christianity. The French missionaries may well have brought lentils to the Americas. A French priest named Father St. John wrote of planting lentils with the Iroquois Indians of the St. Lawrence River Valley. By 1774 lentils had made their way south to the British colony of Virginia, where American gardener-patriot Thomas Jefferson planted them at his home, Monticello.

Lentils took nearly 150 years to reach the Palouse, a region in eastern Washington State and western Idaho. During World War I (1914–1918), a traveling Seventh-Day Adventist minister named Schultz gave some lentils to J. J. Wagner, a local farmer. Soon he and a neighboring farmer were growing and selling lentils to grocery wholesalers and retail stores in the Spokane, Washington, area. These farmers, as well as most of the final

Festive Lentils

Since 1988 the citizenry of Pullman, Washington, have come together at the end of August to celebrate the area's lovely legume. The National Lentil Festival starts with the Taste T. Lentil 5K Fun Run. The finishers chow down at the Lentil Pancake Breakfast.

The float-filled Grand Parade follows, and at least one of the floats features people in lentil costumes. The parade finishes at the Lentil Lane Food Court. Here lentil lovers can feast on lentil tacos or lentil pizza and top off the meal with lentil cake and lentil ice cream.

consumers, were from German-Russian immigrant communities with strong lentil-eating traditions. By the late 1930s, lentils had become a key commercial crop in the Palouse. Some 40 years later, lentils were economically important in western Canada—particularly in the provinces of Saskatchewan, Manitoba, and Alberta.

Growing Lentils

In India, where the Hindu majority is vegetarian, lentils have always been in favor. From the earliest time, farmers have grown multiple varieties of lentils. These days Indians grow, eat, and export more than 50 different kinds of lentils. Indians eat about five pounds of lentils per person per year. By contrast, the average U.S. resident eats less than a quarter of a pound per year.

India grows about 800,000 tons of lentils per year, more than half the world's supply. And even then, the country still needs more lentils, which it usually imports from Turkey. A big (but declining) producer, Turkey eats much of its own harvest of about 600,000 tons per year. Canada is the world's largest exporter of lentils, each year selling more than 280,000 tons abroad, with Colombia, Spain, Belgium, and Italy buying the most. Australia is becoming an increasingly important supplier of lentils as well.

Lentils are usually grown on "dry land"—places with adequate rainfall that don't need irrigation. Between late March and late May, farmers in a few northwestern areas of the United States and Canada plant their lentil seeds, usually pretreated with fungicide to combat disease. Tractor attachments called drills push the seed about 1½ to 2 inches deep in rows about 6 inches apart. The drills often leave ridges of

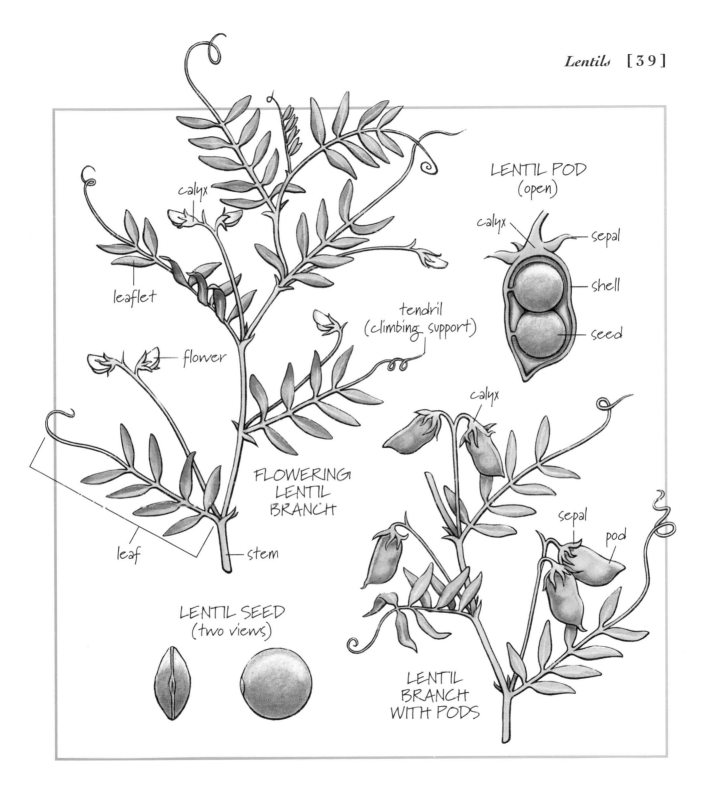

LENTIL POD
(open)

calyx

sepal

shell

seed

calyx

leaflet

tendril
(climbing support)

flower

FLOWERING
LENTIL
BRANCH

leaf

stem

sepal

pod

LENTIL SEED
(two views)

LENTIL
BRANCH
WITH PODS

soil in the field, so farmers use rollers to smooth the ground. At harvesttime, ridges of soil in the path of the combine could bury the tiny plants, which only grow 8 to 16 inches tall. After roughly 120 days in the ground, the plants are ready for harvest.

The plant's vines are usually allowed to die and turn brown at harvesttime. Farmers harvest the legumes with large combines that have a specialized bar with "fingers" designed to lift and cut the vines. The combine separates the lentils from their pods and spreads the nitrate-rich stems and leaves back over the field. Waiting trucks periodically receive loads of lentils from the combine's hopper. The trucks carry the lentils to processing plants where workers clean, sort, and pack the tiny pulses into 100-pound burlap bags for shipment to market.

After the lentil crop has been harvested in the fall, many growers immediately plant their fields in wheat. The soil, rich with plowed-under lentil plants, is ready to go with no additional preparation.

Farmers in India have grown lentils for thousands of years.

Lunch on Lentils

Many people first think of soup when they think of lentils. North Americans are apt to make their lentil soup with carrots, tomatoes, and potatoes, as well as bacon, ham hocks, and sometimes sausage. A similar soup, the favorite Friday meal of the famous Spanish literary character Don Quixote, is popular in central Spain. Armenians make lentil soup with apricots and eggplant. The French add a hearty amount of white wine. Turks include spinach and rosemary, Germans put in cut-up frankfurters, and Syrians use lemon juice in their lentil soup.

To Your Health!

Full of fiber and protein, lentils also contain iron, which enables the blood to carry oxygen, and folic acid, which aids in producing red blood cells. Lentils are packed with potassium, too—a mineral that helps regulate the body's fluid balance.

People around the world make lentil soup with a wide variety of ingredients.

It's a Fact!

The processed-food business is looking at lentils to provide tasty, protein-filled snack chips and crackers. Research projects are under way to make lentils into "extruded" snack foods—snacks made from pulverized materials squirted into a mold.

While some may consider the lentil best fit for soup, others eat boiled or baked lentils alongside meat. A Lebanese side dish combines red lentils with onions, tomatoes, cilantro, and cumin. In other Middle Eastern countries, people cook lentils with green peppers and fried onions and serve them with bulgur wheat (dehydrated, cracked wheat).

Bulgarians favor a stew that mixes hot red chili peppers, lentils, and beans. *Yesmesirkik,* a lentil stew from Ethiopia, has more than 12 spices. Throughout much of South America, people stew lentils with *chorizo,* a highly seasoned sausage. In parts of Mexico, lentils share the stew pot with such fruits as pineapples, bananas, or peaches. In France people commonly eat a salad made of cold lentils.

The people of India create all manner of dishes with lentils, the most famous of which is dal. The word *dal* means "pulse" or "legume" but also refers to a purée, or finely mashed mixture, of spices and lentils. People make dal from many lentil varieties (or sometimes with beans), adding oil, ginger, chilies, cilantro, cumin, and other seasonings.

More specialized lentil dishes from India include *chirupayaru payasam,* lentils cooked with brown sugar, cardamom, coconut milk, and ghee (melted and filtered butter). Indians from the southern state of Kerala fix this dish for a rice festival called Onam. For the Hindu celebration of Holi in northern India, people mix lentils with onions and green chilies, form them into patties called *wada,* and deep-fry them.

A similar snack called *pianju* is made in India's neighboring country Bangladesh. People often eat the patties to break the fast during the Muslim holiday of Ramadan.

During the entire month of Ramadan, which marks the Muslim new year, faithful Muslims fast—that is, they do not eat at all—from sunrise to sunset.

Dig In!

Dal with Coconut
(4 servings)

1 cup red lentils
2½ cups cold water
½ teaspoon turmeric
1 teaspoon fresh ginger,
   peeled and coarsely chopped
½ cup chopped onion
Pinch of salt
1 tablespoon butter
3 tablespoons dried coconut
2–4 cups cooked rice

Put the lentils in a pan, add the water, and bring to a boil. Use a spoon to remove any froth that rises to the surface. Add the turmeric, ginger, onion, and salt. Simmer for 10 more minutes, or until the lentils are almost tender. The water should be almost completely absorbed. Cover the pan and turn the heat down low.

Meanwhile melt the butter in a small pan over low to medium heat and stir in the coconut. Cook gently, stirring, until the coconut turns a rich brown. Put the dal in a serving dish, sprinkle with the coconut, and serve with the rice.

Peas

[*Pisum sativum*]

"Pease porridge hot, pease porridge cold, pease porridge in the pot, nine days old" goes the old English
rhyme. By the tenth day, the entire household must
have been plenty tired of peas. As ancient a food as any,
peas descended from an ancestral Asian plant that has
long since disappeared. Some scientists think the cold-
thriving pea plant originated in India—the word *pea*
itself comes from Sanskrit, the classical language of
India. Archaeologists have found dried peas almost
11,000 years old in the area between Myanmar and
Thailand. Other ancient sites where peas have been
found are all cooler northern areas—Switzerland,
Britain, northern Greece, and northern France.

Freshly picked peas nestle inside their pods.

Visualize whirled peas.

—Contemporary bumper
sticker

Dried split peas are still a wintertime staple for people in cool climates.

It's a Fact!

The word *pea* came about because people started thinking that the Old English singular word *pease* was a plural word, so *pea* must be the singular form.

The peas at all these sites were dried peas, used in soups and stews for thousands of years. While some people across the ages may have eaten peas fresh, most peas were dried. Drab, stodgy, cold-weather fare, dried peas nobly served in times of famine or when grain stores were not plentiful. Peas fed the masses, but they were not, shall we say, fun.

Perhaps the Frankish king Charlemagne, who in about the year A.D. 800 urged pea planting in his French domains, ate them fresh. The English have certainly been growing peas in their gardens since the late 1400s, and English peasants may have been eating peas fresh as well as dried by 1555. During the Renaissance (1300–1600), Italian plant breeders developed the first garden pea especially meant to be eaten fresh. They called these peas *piselli novelli,* or "new peas." Ready early in spring and boiled very briefly, these delicious green delicacies changed the pea's reputation. The new peas were light, colorful, bright—emerald marbles, fanciful finger food.

In 1533 Catherine de Médicis, a member of a prominent Italian family, went to France to marry King Henry II. She brought with her a slew of vegetables improved by Italian plant breeding, including piselli novelli. But the new pea didn't catch on with the general populace.

The French finally embraced peas around 1695, when a member of the royal court, recently returned from Genoa, Italy, presented a large basket of peas to King Louis XIV at Versailles, his palace just outside Paris. The palace chef cooked the peas perfectly and then doled them out to the king's inner circle. Sublime green peas wowed the court, and the king ate himself sick. When he recovered, Louis immediately put his head gardener to the task of growing peas in the royal greenhouses. The "in" crowd at Versailles told all their friends about fresh green peas, and the craze was on. The French, in fact, gave the pea the name by which it is known and grown all over the world: *petits pois,* or "little peas." New peas, little peas, whatever you please, but make them fresh peas.

The chef also steamed some of the peas unshelled and topped them with a special sauce that was meant to be licked from the pod.

King Louis XIV of France and the members of his court spurred a fresh-green-pea fad in the late seventeenth century.

Thomas Jefferson's garden at Monticello provided him with peas in the springtime, an event that he noted in his diary in 1774.

Peas in the Americas

Christopher Columbus probably brought peas to the Western Hemisphere, to Cape Isabela (in modern-day Dominican Republic) in 1493. Somewhat later, the Spaniards carried peas with them into Mexico and Florida, where native peoples were cultivating them by the beginning of the 1600s. The British colonists in Virginia were eating peas in 1608, and in 1629, settlers boasted a fine crop of peas in the governor's garden at Plymouth. Unfortunately, British colonists settling the Carolinas in about 1670 almost starved to death on a ration of one pint of peas per day per person and little else. The future president of the United States, Thomas Jefferson, grew peas—a personal favorite—at his home in Virginia in 1767. At one time, he planted 30 different varieties.

Domesticated Plants

For thousands of years, people lived on foods that grew naturally in the wild. Then, for reasons difficult to pinpoint, many food plants became domesticated, or brought under human control. Some scientists say that an increase in population led people to settle in one place and plant food in prepared plots. Others theorize that people may have settled while continuing to gather wild foods. In any event, ancient peoples began to plant wild seeds. At harvesttime, they saved some of the best seeds for the next planting. Many plants in different parts of the world became domesticated at the same time—about 10,000 years ago.

(Left, from left to right) Petits pois, sugar snap peas, and snow peas. A pea patch blooms in a backyard garden *(below)*.

Pea Types

There are many kinds of fresh peas. Snow peas often turn up in Chinese stir-fry dishes. They are bright green, flat pods in which the peas are little more than tiny seeds. Sugar snaps have edible pods, too, but the peas inside are fully grown. Peas with edible pods are known throughout much of the world as mangetout, a French-derived word that literally means "eat all." Petits pois are the small, fresh peas.

Pea Planting, Picking, and Packing

Farmers grow dry peas similarly to lentils, planting and harvesting with identical machines. Fresh peas destined for canning or freezing are harvested by combines that strip the pods off the vine and then separate the peas from their shells. To maintain freshness, many pea farmers harvest and process within one hour. Peas sold in the pod are more delicate. To avoid damaging the vegetable, farmworkers often harvest these peas by hand or with simple, one-row pickers.

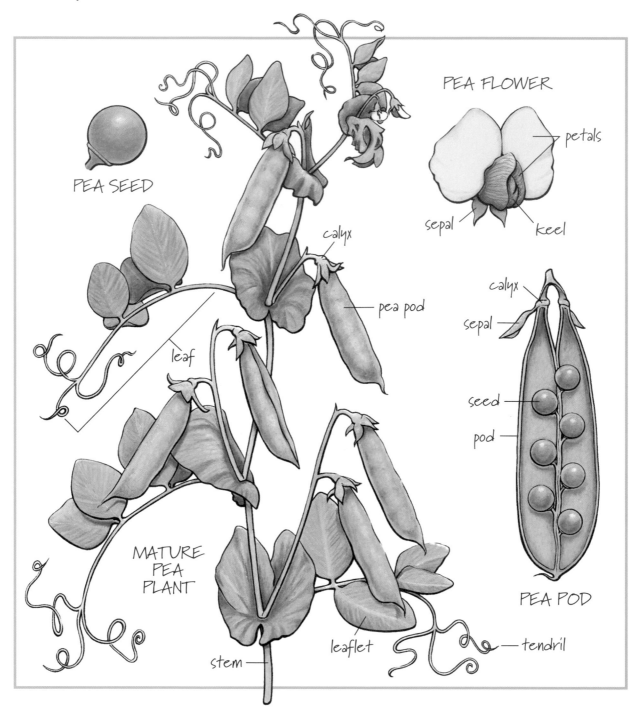

PEA SEED

PEA FLOWER

petals

sepal

keel

calyx

pea pod

calyx

sepal

seed

pod

leaf

MATURE
PEA
PLANT

PEA POD

stem

leaflet

tendril

Peas deteriorate rapidly after picking. Only peas eaten by a gardener standing in the pea patch early in spring are truly fresh. The "fresh" peas in supermarkets are at least three to four days old. Commercial peas picked and shelled in the field must be frozen or canned within three to four hours. To freeze peas, workers blanch (dip briefly into boiling water) the legumes to kill parasites and then chill the peas to a temperature of zero degrees. Canned peas, on the other hand, cook right in the can at a high temperature for about 20 minutes. It's no surprise, then, that frozen peas keep their color and taste far better than canned peas do.

To Your Health!

Like all members of the legume family, peas contain a hefty amount of protein. Protein is the body's basic building material, and it supports every body function. Two-thirds of a cup of peas have almost as much protein as a large egg. Peas have no fat, and they're packed with minerals, fiber—which improves lower intestinal performance—and vitamins. In fact, peas are the richest food source of vitamin B_1, which helps cells unlock the energy in food.

Give Peas a Chance

To eat fresh peas, briefly boil or steam them and serve them plain or with butter. The French cook fresh peas with lettuce and onions in water and then daub the peas with butter to create *petits pois frais à la française*. Cooks toss frozen peas into Chinese stir-fries and Thai curries, often pairing the legumes with shrimp. In Seville, Spain, people ladle peas on top of the classic dish *huevos a la flamenca*, a meat dish topped with baked eggs. In a similar dish from Portugal, coriander-flavored peas surround the eggs. In Valencia, Spain, people sprinkle fresh peas in the classic rice dish called paella. Large quantities of fresh peas frequently accompany lamb dishes in Persian (ancient Iranian) cooking.

Dried peas go into soups and stews. Pea soup with bacon, and puréed yellow peas with carrots and celery are standard dishes in Germany. Danish, Dutch, and North American people make a similar rich pea soup. A shrimp stew from Peru always calls for a minimum of one cup of peas. A Brazilian version of chicken couscous (pasta pellets), *cuscuz de galinha*, demands two cups.

Bird Food

Chickpeas (*Cicer arietinem*), sometimes called garbanzo beans, are related to peas and beans but stand alone. These pulses do indeed resemble a tiny chick with a beak. Originally from western Asia, chickpeas are the primary legume grown and eaten in India. Indians produce more than 5 million tons of chickpeas per year, but the country imports still more from Australia and Turkey. The chickpea also grows in several Middle Eastern countries, where hummus—made from chickpeas, garlic, tahini (sesame-seed paste), and lemon juice—is a popular spread. Eaten in Spain, Italy, Brazil, and Venezuela, too, chickpeas are gaining popularity in the United States.

Pigeon peas (*Cajanus cajan*)—also called Congo peas, goongoo peas, or gandule beans—originated in Africa but are grown in India and the West Indies, too. The small, yellow peas are cooked like beans, and they turn up in several Caribbean and Latin American dishes. A typical Puerto Rican dish is gandule rice. It combines the beans with olives and spices including annatto seed, which gives the dish a yellowish-red color, and cilantro.

Dig In!

YELLOW SPLIT PEA SOUP
(4—6 SERVINGS)

6 cups water
1 cup yellow dried split peas
1 bay leaf
1 medium yellow or white onion, finely diced
3 cloves garlic, pressed or minced
2 tablespoons corn oil or extra-virgin olive oil
2 carrots, peeled and finely diced, and/or 3
  tomatoes, diced medium
1 stalk celery, finely diced
½ teaspoon black pepper
¾ teaspoon salt, or to taste
1 tablespoon minced fresh marjoram or cilantro

In a large saucepan or stockpot, bring the water to a boil. Add the split peas and stir to prevent sticking. When the water begins boiling again, skim off any foam and reduce the heat. Add the bay leaf, cover the pot, and simmer until the split peas are very soft and mealy, about 2 to 2½ hours.

In a medium-sized, heavy-bottomed saucepan over medium heat, sauté the onion and garlic in the oil until golden brown. Add the carrots (and/or tomatoes) and continue to cook until they are almost tender, about 5 minutes. Add this mixture to the cooked split peas. Stir in the celery and cook until it turns bright green. Season the soup with pepper, salt, and marjoram or cilantro. Serve immediately.

This soup can be kept covered in the refrigerator for one day, but it will need to be reseasoned before serving.

Beans

[Phaseolus; Vicia faba;
Vigna; Glycine max]

If you don't know beans, you don't know much, right? Well, not necessarily. Hundreds, probably thousands, of varieties of beans grow throughout the world. Eaten fresh, eaten dried, eaten everywhere, eaten every day, beans are among the most nutritious vegetables. The largest bean grouping is *Phaseolus*, which contains most of the commonly eaten varieties. *Vicia faba*—the fava or broad bean—and Asian beans of the genus *Vigna* are minor players in the world bean scheme. The soybean, *Glycine max*, feeds people and animals and supports industry across the globe.

These multicolored beans were grown to be sold at a farmer's market in Ecuador.

I was determined to know beans.

—Henry David Thoreau

The city of Lima, for which Lima beans are named, is the capital of the mountainous South American nation of Peru.

The beans most familiar to North Americans all fall under the genus *Phaseolus*. Four species in this grouping were first domesticated in the Americas: *Phaseolus lunatus,* or lima beans; *Phaseolus vulgaris,* a huge grouping that includes almost all the everyday beans we eat; *Phaseolus coccineus,* the scarlet runner bean; and finally, *Phaseolus acutifolius,* the tepary bean.

Lima beans are named for Lima, Peru. Scientists have found limas more than 8,000 years old in that part of South America. The *Phaseolus vulgaris* gang, too, grew in present-day Peru before 6000 B.C. and in Mexico 1,000 years later. This group includes varieties of beans that, depending on when they're harvested, can be eaten dry or fresh—green, wax, kidney, pinto, black, red, cranberry, Anasazi, and hundreds of others. Beans from this broad category are known as haricots.

Christopher Columbus probably encountered haricots in what we call Cuba shortly before 1500. Spanish explorers came across haricots in Mexico in 1519, and in 1528, the Spanish explorer Álvar Núñez Cabeza de Vaca noted them in Florida, too. Native farmers all over the Americas—from wet, chilly, northeastern North America to the deserts of Mexico—could grow some variety of the adaptable haricot bean. Travelers brought haricots from the Americas to Italy in 1528. Soon the beans grew in gardens in Tuscany, a region of northern Italy, and from there they moved to other parts of Europe.

A native Mexican plant, the edible scarlet runner bean usually grows as an ornamental. In 1634 the gardener of the English king Charles I probably brought the plant home from colonial Virginia. These beans had exquisite flowers and could climb 12 to 14 feet, covering imperfections on garden walls.

The ancient peoples of the American Southwest relied upon the drought-resistant tepary bean as least as early as 3000 B.C. The Pima and Papago Indians of Arizona still grow it. When Spanish explorers first saw this plant in 1699, they asked the Papago, whom they called the Bean People, what it was called. *"T'pawi,"* the farmers answered, which translates to, "it is a bean." To Spanish ears, *t'pawi* sounded like *tepary*, the name by which we know this plant. The tepary is of great interest to scientists seeking plants that can thrive in desert climates.

Here are a few of the numerous varieties of haricot beans, starting at bottom right, moving clockwise: purple wax beans, flageolets *(scattered)*, red kidney *(scattered)*, great northern, cranberry, cannellini, black, scarlet runner *(scattered)*, pinto, and green beans *(center)*.

Although the bulk of the world's beans are of the *Phaseolus* genus, there are other beans around the globe, too. The fava bean, *Vicia faba,* resembles a large lima bean and may be the only bean that originated in Europe. Knowledge of the fava's original ancestor is lost in the mists of time. Early in prehistory, fava plants were growing in two areas—North Africa and the Mediterranean, and Persia (present-day Iran) or farther east into Asia. The bean made its way into parts of Asia and throughout Europe as well. The ancient Egyptians, Hebrews, and Greeks cultivated and ate favas. These days favas are popular in Italy, Spain, and the Middle East.

The *Vigna* beans were probably domesticated in Asia. They include adzuki, moth, urd, mung, and rice beans. Incidentally, mung beans are the bean sprouts commonly used in Asian cooking.

In ancient Greece, voters used fava beans as tokens, perhaps dropping the beans into separate boxes labeled with each candidate's name.

When sprouted, mung beans—or any legume—have a much higher vitamin content than the plain dried pulses.

Soybean plants produce mature pods containing three beans each *(inset)*.

Super Soy

The soybean *(Glycine max)* is the superstar among beans. Probably a native of northern China, the soybean feeds people as well as or better than any other food on earth—soy contains three times as much protein as wheat or corn. It also provides oil, soap, diesel fuel, glue, and plastic.

In 2700 or 2800 B.C., the Chinese emperor Shen Nung named wild soybeans, along with domesticated rice, millet, wheat, and barley, as one of five "sacred foods." Some scholars believe that the Chinese did not domesticate soybeans for another thousand years.

As the Chinese moved into parts of Southeast Asia, they took the domesticated bean with them. Chinese Buddhist monks, who do not eat any animal foods, are credited with introducing the soybean into Korea and Japan. Some historians say this occurred around 200 B.C., but others opt for a much later date, in the A.D. 500s. The Chinese most likely brought soybeans to Indonesia by A.D. 1000.

Kew Gardens in southwestern London was established in 1759 as a place to grow plants for scientific and educational purposes.

Throughout Asia the soybean was prized early on, but knowledge of the pulse's travels beyond Asia is sketchy. In the late 1400s, Portuguese and Dutch sailors doing business in China and Japan mentioned the bean in their journals but gave no indication that they'd taken the soybean back to Europe. Engelbert Kämpfer, a German botanist, described soy dishes in a book about his travels in Japan in the 1690s. An Italian contemporary of Kämpfer also wrote of soy dishes he had eaten in the ancient city of Beijing, still China's capital. Sometime during the 1730s, Christian missionaries probably brought soybeans to Europe. There the beans appeared in private gardens as botanical curiosities. Soy plants turned up in Paris's famous garden, the Jardin des Plantes, by 1739 and were on display in Britain's Kew Gardens in 1790.

U. S. sailors departing from China in 1804 loaded a Yankee clipper ship with soybeans as ballast. As was typical with ballast, the beans were most likely tossed overboard after the ship arrived in the United States. One source, however, states that some soybeans were grown in Pennsylvania that same year. Somewhat later, in 1829, a U.S. farming magazine mentioned soybeans. From that time on, U.S. farmers grew soybeans on a limited basis.

During the U.S. Civil War, soldiers used soybeans as a coffee substitute when the real thing was tough to obtain. By the 1880s, people were feeding the beans to animals. Even so, soybeans on display during the 1893 Chicago World's Fair were still a curiosity.

Empty or lightly loaded ships have to carry ballast—a dense, usually cheap, cargo that provides the weight and balance required for steady sailing.

Spectators at the Chicago World's Fair of 1893 could see soybeans in the Agriculture Building *(background)*.

In contrast to the soybean's minor U.S. role, Asian nations were going to war over soybean supplies. In 1894 the Japanese attacked China's center of soybean production—Manchuria, a region in northeastern China bordering Russia. Soon the Japanese controlled the Manchurian port of Newchwang (these days called Yingkou). Four years later, the Japanese fought Russia for another former Chinese soy port, Dairen (modern Dalian). The Japanese won again and began shipping tons of soybeans to Britain, where soy oil was used in soap and for cooking.

A Japanese woodcut depicts a clash between Japanese and Chinese soldiers during the two nations' war over Manchuria, a soybean-producing region.

Meanwhile, soybeans remained obscure in the United States. Not just a devotee of peanuts, George Washington Carver planted soybeans at Tuskegee Institute in 1904 to satisfy his own curiosity. Carver found that soybeans produced both oil and protein, and he began promoting the growing of the bean for more than feeding animals. The U.S. Department of Agriculture (USDA) began to investigate soybeans in 1907 but made little headway at first.

But by 1929 the USDA had sent a scientist named William Morse on a soy search to China and elsewhere in Asia. Morse returned two years later with more than 2,000 different varieties of soybeans. Morse believed firmly that people, not only animals, should eat soybeans. So did the U.S. automobile pioneer Henry Ford. Ford grew soybeans near his auto plants in Michigan. He ate soybeans cooked in many ways, and he urged his engineers to create auto parts from soy plastic. For a few years, Ford cars contained about two pounds of soy-based products, including gearshift knobs, window frames, and pedals. The company once unveiled a prototype car with an exterior built entirely from soy plastic.

Henry Ford also experimented with soy textiles. In 1937 Ford scientists were the first to spin fiber from vegetable protein. The technicians combined soy meal with chemicals to make a tarlike substance. Then a

Henry Ford, the founder of the Ford Motor Company, was responsible for many improvements to the automobiles of his time.

machine called a spinneret squeezed the tar into long strands of thread that could be woven into cloth suitable for car interiors. Ford never used the cloth in his cars, but he owned two soy-fiber suits.

When the United States entered World War II (1939–1945), U.S. scientists set aside soy as an industrial superstar, even though the need for materials made from non-petroleum sources was immense. However, the nation did turn to the soybean for edible oil, since the war abruptly halted European oil imports. The Germans made great use of soybeans during the war, primarily as food products.

After World War II, soybeans became a major crop in the American Midwest (the area around the Great Lakes and the Upper Mississippi River stretching from Ohio to the Dakotas, Nebraska, and Kansas), where they continue to be grown in rotation with corn. For reasons not fully known, a field planted in soybeans one year and corn the next will produce much higher yields than a field where only one crop is repeatedly sown.

During and after World War II, many U.S. farmers began growing soy on a large scale. To prepare for his first planting of soybeans, a man doses his seeds with a nitrate-producing bacteria that is normally found on the plant's roots. The treatment will improve growth by establishing the bacteria, plentiful in soil where soybeans have grown for a long time, in the new field.

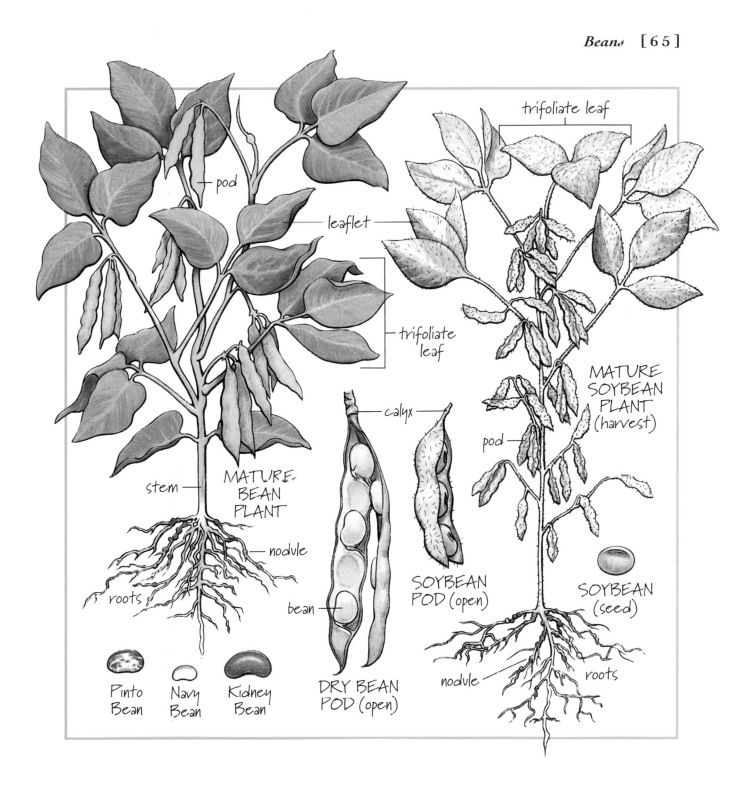

trifoliate leaf

pod

leaflet

trifoliate leaf

MATURE
SOYBEAN
PLANT
(harvest)

calyx

pod

stem

MATURE-
BEAN
PLANT

nodule

bean

roots

SOYBEAN
POD (open)

SOYBEAN
(seed)

Pinto
Bean

Navy
Bean

Kidney
Bean

DRY BEAN
POD (open)

nodule

roots

Dig In!

When haricot beans are eaten as immature pods, they're called snap beans. Fresh pods make a brisk snapping sound when broken in half. They're a snap to grow, too, especially if you plant them in the spring when outside temperatures reach 50 to 60 degrees. Plant yellow, green, or even purple beans an inch deep in moist, well-worked soil. For bush beans, which grow like a small shrub, keep about 2 inches between each seed and dig rows 18 inches apart. Plant pole beans around tall stakes or bamboo poles, on trellises (frames), or near fences—anywhere they can climb. Pole beans need more space, so place the seeds about 6 inches apart in rows 3 feet wide. You can also plant bush or pole beans in flowerpots, placing one or two beans in each large container.

Keep the soil moist until seedlings appear, and water them frequently as they grow. Look for beans soon after the flowers appear—within 60 to 90 days of planting—and make sure you pick the beans young, well before you can see the seeds bulge inside the pods. To clean the beans, snap about half an inch off each end and rinse them well. The water that clings to the beans is all you need for cooking. Put the still-wet beans into a saucepan with a tight lid and steam them on medium-high heat for a few minutes until tender.

Growing and Harvesting

All beans are grown in the same way, and there's a bean variety for nearly every climate and soil type. In May or June, drills (air-powered planters) sow beans about 1½ inches apart, with about 20 to 30 inches between rows.

Dry beans are ready to harvest in late summer or early fall when the entire plant turns brown. Harvest is best when the pods still have enough moisture so they don't shatter and scatter their seeds as they are being cut. A bean combine cuts down the plants and carries the pods up inside. The machine separates the beans and sends them into a hopper, which empties into trucks. The trucks take the beans to the processing plants, where they are cleaned, sorted, and packaged—either for the supermarket or to be sold to canners and other food makers.

Bean Powers

China is the world's biggest exporter of dry beans (excluding soy), and Myanmar is number two. North Dakota and Michigan are the top U.S. bean producers, with Nebraska and California sharing third place. And although total bean consumption hasn't risen in the United States, more people are eating beans. Perhaps because of the growth in the Hispanic population, pinto beans are making huge gains on great northerns and navy beans, once America's favorites.

An Illinois farmer harvests soybeans with a combine *(above)*. The combine dumps the beans into a truck *(below)*.

The Winged Bean

Soybeans don't grow well in the **tropics,** but a possible alternative is the winged bean (*Psophocarpus tetragoonolobus*). Long cultivated on New Guinea, an island to the north of Australia, the winged bean has as much protein as the soybean. What's more, people can eat the entire plant—stems, flowers, pods, and all.

A Chinese farmer cleans harvested soybeans by hand.

Many people think of Japan or China when they think of soybeans. But the United States is the world's biggest grower, responsible for about half of all soybeans grown. Climate has something to do with this success. Soybeans are well suited to the hot, moderately dry summers of the American Midwest. Twenty-nine U.S. states together produced more than 71 million tons of soybeans in 1996. Iowa, Illinois, and Indiana lead the U.S. producers. Japan is the biggest customer of U.S. soybeans, and Taiwan is the second biggest. China buys the most U.S. soybean oil, and Canada is the largest buyer of U.S. soy meal, which is used for animal feed.

Brazil is the world's second-largest soy power. In the country's **temperate** areas, farmers provide 20 percent of the world's soybeans. China is in third place at 10 percent, with Argentina close behind.

Eating Beans

A standard New England dish, baked beans are usually made from small white or yellow beans cooked with salt pork or ham and sweetened with molasses, brown sugar, or syrup. Native Americans were eating baked beans long before any European colonists filled up their first pot, although English folk had long baked dry peas with pork back home. It's likely that early Puritan settlers watched Narragansett and Penobscot Indian women add maple syrup to their beans and did the same. On Saturday nights, the settlers often served up hot beans with brown bread made from cornmeal and molasses. They ate the leftovers cold for breakfast the next morning. Bostonians followed this custom so as to obey the Puritan rule of not cooking on Sundays. Boston is still nicknamed Beantown.

Boston has grown since its days as a colonial town, but the city is still famous for its baked beans *(inset)*.

To Your Health!

All beans are powerhouses of protein, fiber, and iron. But the soybean is so packed with punch that health experts write entire books about its benefits. Known to the Chinese as "the meat without bones," the soybean has as much protein as, but less fat than, most meats. Soy is high in fiber and full of minerals and most of the B vitamins—it's one of the most balanced foods in our diet.

On the medicinal front, too, soybeans score high. Soy has substances that help the body to eliminate toxins and to combat infection. Anti-cancer compounds found in soy are especially effective against lung, colon, prostate, ovarian, and breast cancers. Soy appears to help retain bone mass and to prevent osteoporosis (brittle bones). And people with high levels of cholesterol who begin eating just two ounces of soy products a day may soon experience a dramatic drop in cholesterol levels.

Similarly, Italians from Tuscany are sometimes called "bean eaters." Since the 1500s, Tuscans have eaten beans on a daily basis. One of the most famous Tuscan dishes is *zuppa di fagioli con pasta*—white bean soup made with ham and pasta.

People pair beans and rice throughout much of the world. In New Orleans, Louisiana, households use their Sunday ham bone, Tabasco sauce, and lots of garlic to cook red beans and rice on Monday. Refried beans—boiled pinto beans mashed and fried with lard or vegetable oil—accompany rice

In Tuscany, a region of west central Italy, beans are a favorite food.

A woman from Guatemala in Central America pours newly harvested black beans from a basket. The wind will remove bits of dirt and plant material as the beans fall.

throughout Mexico and the American Southwest. Brazilians serve rice with their national dish, *feijoada*, made from black beans and a combination of meats—a recipe probably borrowed from African cooking. Another South American dish, this one derived from Native American cuisine, is Chile's *porotos granados*, a well-seasoned mix of cranberry beans, squash, and corn.

The Joy of Soy

Asian cooking makes regular use of beans, especially soybeans. But even boiled, soybeans are hard to chew and harder to digest, so Asians transform soy into foods that seem very un-beanlike—soy sauce, tofu, tempeh, and miso.

Salty, flavorful, inky-brown soy sauce appears on the tables of Chinese restaurants

The Legend of Tofu

A Chinese tale relates the story of an honest public official who lived during the Tang dynasty (A.D. 618–907). He refused to take bribes, which most other ill-paid civil servants accepted. As a result, the official was a poor man who could not afford to buy meat. To feed his family, he invented tofu. Some people in China still refer to exceedingly honest government workers as "tofu officials."

everywhere. This brew of roasted soybeans and wheat provides flavoring for countless dishes.

Tofu—a mild-flavored, versatile, cheese-like substance sometimes called bean curd—consists of dried, crushed, boiled, and curdled soybeans. Tofu making is a process thought to be about 2,000 years old. The Chinese, longtime users of soy products, create magnificent stir-fry dishes with tofu, ginger, chilies, green onions, and other vegetables. An everyday meal in Thailand is *pad Thai*, a noodle dish made with thin strips of tofu and flavored with chilies and peanuts. A Thai tomato soup blends tofu, coconut, and hot spices. In Malaysia, people serve *tauhu*

Traditionally made Chinese tofu bears the marks of the basket in which it was pressed into cakes. North Americans are eating more and more tofu and other soy products, often in the form of burgers, hot dogs, and other meat substitutes. Bean curd also shows up in stews, salads, salad dressings, and low-fat desserts.

goreng, tofu cakes with peanut sauce. Malays also eat a spicy coconut curry with sliced tofu.

While many Asian people use tofu as just another ingredient, the Japanese delight in the subtle taste of tofu. They often serve it in clear broth, garnished only with chopped green onions or shaved carrots; or as a single block, sprinkled with grated ginger. Of course, the Japanese also serve tofu with vegetables, sometimes seasoned with rice wine and cooked with egg, or deep-fried and dipped into a seasoned sauce. People like to top steamed vegetables with a dressing made of creamed tofu and tahini.

Japanese family meals frequently include tofu.

A Japanese miso seller offers shoppers a taste of his wares.

Tempeh, a soy product mostly associated with Indonesia and Thailand, dates back 2,000 years. Made from fermented soybeans, tempeh is often used instead of meat in soups, stews, stir-fries, and curries. Indonesians frequently slice tempeh, dip it in a mixture of ground coriander, crushed garlic, and water, and fry it quickly. People also fry tempeh in coconut oil and then serve it plain, wrapped in banana leaves, or skewered and grilled with chilies and onions.

Miso, a paste of fermented soybeans, is the basis of a rich broth eaten almost daily in Japan. Sometimes the Japanese use miso soup to pickle vegetables or to marinate fish. Koreans make a miso they call *jang*, and Indonesians make one called *tao-tjo*.

Cracking the Bean

The soybean is a bean apart. As a source of oil and high-quality protein, soy performs well in food-processing and industrial roles where other beans don't measure up. But soybeans are hard little beans, yielding up their treasures reluctantly. Special machines crack the beans, remove their hulls, and roll them flat so that the oil is easier to extract. Food manufacturers can also make the hulls into breads, cereals, and snacks. The oil-filled flakes go into products as diverse as soy-nut butter and soy coffee. Millers convert the flakes into flour for bakery goods and desserts.

People use soy oil for cooking and salad dressings. Industrial-grade soy oil turns up in lots of products, including wallboard, plastics, shampoos, soaps, glues,

Soybeans are the biggest single source of vegetable oil for the United States.

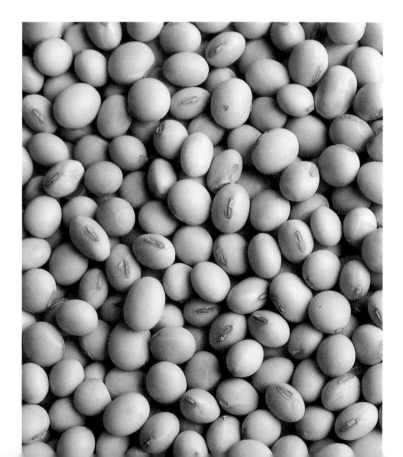

Not only do soybeans provide food, but they're the basis for many industrial products. In fact, soy materials can replace many products—such as plastics and ink—that were once made only from nonrenewable petroleum.

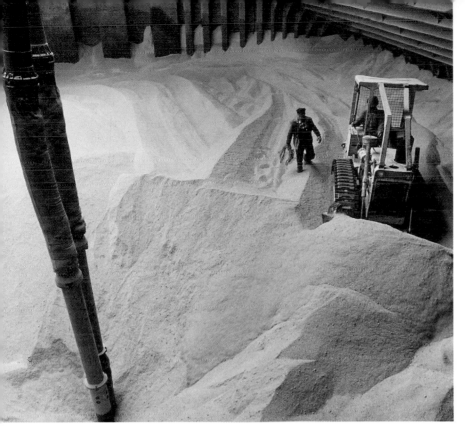

Inside a ship's cargo hold, two workers push soy meal toward a suction pipe during unloading.

and anti-rusting agents, among other products. Makers of pharmaceuticals, baked goods, and candies depend on lecithin, a component of soy oil. For example, lecithin keeps the chocolate in a candy bar from separating into its liquid and solid components. Lecithin also goes into paints, inks, insecticides, and rubber.

After the oil is removed, processors turn soy flakes into a wide range of edible products for people and animals. Many people think they don't eat soy, but they do. For starters, soy turns up in cake mixes, instant cereals, canned pastas, instant breakfast drinks, frozen dinners, fast-food hamburgers, and frozen lasagna.

Eat That Crayon!

Well, you can if the wrapper says Prang Fun Pro Soybean Crayon. Students at Purdue University in Indiana invented the crayon as their entry in a competition designed to develop new soy products. The Dixon Ticonderoga Company produces the nontoxic, nonpetroleum crayons—2,112 of them from every 60 pounds of soybeans. The crayons feature bright colors, no flaking, and smooth flow.

Dig In!

CHINESE STIR-FRY WITH TOFU AND EGG NOODLES
(4–6 SERVINGS)

¼ pound Chinese egg noodles, cooked
peanut oil
1 cup firm tofu, cubed
4 green onions, chopped
2 cups mushrooms, finely sliced
1 carrot, finely sliced
1 cup snow peas
1 cup baby corn

4 to 6 water chestnuts, sliced; or one
can of sliced water chestnuts, drained
1 red bell pepper, sliced
1 cup bean sprouts
2 tablespoons soy sauce
1 to 2 tablespoons lemon juice
1 teaspoon fresh, peeled, grated ginger
salt to taste

Boil the noodles according to the package directions. Heat enough peanut oil to coat a wok or frying pan. Fry the tofu at high heat until golden brown, about 3 minutes. Set both noodles and tofu aside in separate bowls.

Add more oil to the pan or wok, if necessary, and cook the onions for a few minutes until soft. Scatter in the mushrooms, carrot, peas, baby corn, water chestnuts, and pepper and cook for 2 minutes. Next add the bean sprouts and noodles. Mix well and then sprinkle in the soy sauce, lemon juice, ginger, and salt. After one minute, toss in the tofu. Cover the pan or wok and cook briskly at high heat for one more minute. Serve right away.

Glossary

broker: A person who buys and sells goods on behalf of other people or companies.

cash crop: A crop that a farmer grows to sell, rather than to eat.

domestication: Taming animals or adapting plants so they can safely live with or be eaten by humans.

nitrate: One of a group of chemicals, containing nitrogen, that are essential for plant growth.

ornamental: A plant grown for its beauty and not for its food or commercial value.

photosynthesis: The chemical process by which green plants make energy-producing carbohydrates. The process involves the reaction of sunlight to carbon dioxide, water, and nutrients within plant tissues.

pulse: The edible seed of a leguminous plant.

subsistence farmer: A farmer who produces only enough food to feed his or her family.

temperate: Pertaining to a moderate climate zone that falls either between the Tropic of Cancer and the Arctic Circle in the Northern Hemisphere or between the Tropic of Capricorn and the Antarctic Circle in the Southern Hemisphere.

tropics: The hot, wet zone around the earth's equator between the Tropic of Cancer and the Tropic of Capricorn.

Further Reading

Erlbach, Arlene. *Peanut Butter.* Minneapolis: Lerner Publications Company, 1994.

Hill, Lee Sullivan. *Farms Feed the World.* Minneapolis: Carolrhoda Books, Inc., 1997.

Johnson, Sylvia A. *Tomatoes, Potatoes, Corn and Beans: How the Foods of the Americas Changed Eating Around The World.* New York: Atheneum Books for Young Readers, 1997.

Miller, Susanna. *Beans and Peas.* Minneapolis: Carolrhoda Books, Inc., 1990.

Mitchell, Barbara. *A Pocketful of Goobers: A Story about George Washington Carver.* Minneapolis: Carolrhoda Books, Inc., 1986.

Nottridge, Rhoda. *Vitamins.* Minneapolis: Carolrhoda Books, Inc., 1993.

Root, Waverly. *Food.* New York: Simon & Schuster, 1980.

Trager, James. *The Food Chronology.* New York: Henry Holt and Company, 1995.

Vegetarian Cooking around the World. Minneapolis: Lerner Publications Company, 1992.

Wake, Susan. *Vegetables.* Minneapolis: Carolrhoda Books, Inc., 1990.

A Tanzanian farmer checks a crop of pigeon peas.

Index

About the Author

Meredith Sayles Hughes has been writing about food since the mid-1970s, when she and her husband, Tom Hughes, founded The Potato Museum in Brussels, Belgium. She has worked on two major exhibitions about food, one for the Smithsonian and one for the National Museum of Science and Technology in Ottawa, Ontario. Author of several articles on food history, Meredith has collaborated with Tom Hughes on a range of programs, lectures, workshops, and teacher training sessions, as well as *The Great Potato Book*. The Hugheses do exhibits and programs as The FOOD Museum in Albuquerque, New Mexico, where they live with their son, Gulliver.

Acknowledgments

For photographs and artwork: Steve Brosnahan, p. 4; Tennessee State Museum Collection, detail of a painting by Carlyle Urello, p. 7; © Mark Gibson/AGStockUSA, pp. 11, 46, 59; © Sean Sprague/Panos Pictures, p. 13; Archive Photos, pp. 14, 17, 36, 47; Corbis-Bettmann, pp. 15, 34, 62, 63, 70; North Carolina Archives, p. 16; © Dr. Deborah Pellow, p. 18; United Nations, p. 19; © Holly Kuper/AGStockUSA, p. 22 (both); © Karlene V. Schwartz, pp. 23, 37 (inset), 49 (bottom), 68 (top); Jimmy Carter Library, p. 24; © Jeff Greenberg/Photo Researchers, Inc., p. 26; © Walt & Louiseann Pietrowicz/September 8th Stock, pp. 25, 31, 33, 41, 43, 49 (top), 53, 57, 58, 69 (inset), 76; © Liba Taylor/Panos Pictures, p. 27; © Betty Press/Panos Pictures, p. 28; Hershey Foods Corp., p. 29; courtesy of Dr. Robert E. Rouse, IFAS/Southwest Florida Research Center, p. 30 (both); Neil Strassberg/Archive Photos, p. 35; © Thomas Dodge/AGStockUSA, p. 37; Pullman Chamber of Commerce, p. 38; © Dana Downie/AGStockUSA, p. 40; © Ed Young/AGStockUSA, p. 45; © R. Perron, p. 48; © D. Donne Bryant/DDB Stock Photography, pp. 55, 71; © Georg Gerster/Photo Researchers, Inc., p. 56; © Bill Barksdale/AGStockUSA, p. 59 (inset); Royal Botanic Gardens, Kew, p. 60; IPS, p. 61; Underwood & Underwood/Corbis-Bettmann, p. 64; © Howard Ande, p. 67 (both); © Chris Johns/Tony Stone Images, p. 68 (bottom); Joe Sohm/Photo Researchers, Inc., p. 69; © Mark Anderson, p. 72; © Wayne Eastep/Tony Stone Images, p. 73 (top); © TRIP/Christopher Rennie, p. 73 (bottom); © Russ Munn/AGStockUSA, p. 74; © Michael Rosenfeld/Tony Stone Images, p. 75; © Phil Porter, p. 78. Sidebar and back cover artwork by John Erste. All other artwork by Laura Westlund. Cover photo by Steve Foley and Réna Dehler.

For quoted material: p. 4, M. F. K. Fisher, *The Art Of Eating* (New York: Macmillan General Reference, 1990); p. 10, March Egerton, ed., *Since Eve Ate Apples: Quotations of Feasting, Fasting, and Food—from the Beginning* (Portland, Oregon: Tsunami Press, 1994); p. 32, as quoted by Diana Kennedy in *The Art of Mexican Cooking: Traditional Mexican Cooking for Aficionados* (New York: Bantam Books, 1989); p. 54, Henry David Thoreau, *Walden*, 1854, as quoted by John Bartlett, *Familiar Quotations*, 13th edition (Boston: Little Brown, 1955).

For recipes (some slightly adapted for kids): p. 31, Barbara Karoff, *South American Cooking: Foods and Feasts from the New World* (Reading, MA: Aris Books, 1989); pp. 43, 76, reprinted with permission from *The World in Your Kitchen* by Troth Wells © 1993, The Crossing Press: Freedom, CA. All rights reserved; p. 53, reprinted with permission from *Cooking at The Natural Café in Santa Fe* by Lynn Walters © 1992, The Crossing Press: Freedom, CA. All rights reserved.